VOLUME 5

The Unconventional CEO's Destiny

DOWN WITH THE CONVENTIONAL –

LET UN-COMMON SENSE TRIUMPH!

MARIO PRETORIUS

First Edition, 2023

ISBN: 978-1-77605-781-8

Produced by Kwarts Publishers
www.kwartspublishers.co.za

Contact the author:
Mario Pretorius www.mariopretorius.co.za
Mobile: +27 836412000 ceo@capitalcorp.co.za

A man is not
finished when he
is defeated.

He is finished
when he quits.

CONTENTS

Introduction   ix

Author's Biography   x

Dedication   xi

Dear CEO   xii

1. Reconstituted Pirates   1
2. The Hard Yards   2
3. Can you afford your employees?   3
4. Story telling   4
5. Hormesis   5
6. Clear risks   6
7. Is Risk-taking a Bug?   7
8. Honesty settings   9
9. What is 'fundamental' to your organization?   10
10. Nature is chaos   12
11. Replacement theory   13
12. Motivation rests on the ability to endure   14
13. NCO vs Officers   15
14. Cross-selling and other fantasies   16
15. Knowing about vs. Understanding   17
16. Keep away from ABSOLUTISM at the edges   18
17. Set the frame before you launch into a topic   19
18. Moving targets of return   20
19. Changing the past   22
20. Survive-ability not sustainability   23
21. The need for plane crashes   24
22. Make it, don't look for it   25
23. Learn to serve first   26
24. Test for character by asking for unrehearsed responses   27
25. Price's Law, square root of x is 50%.   28
26. Keanu games   30
27. Get high resolution model of complex problems before attempting answers   31

28. Non-Similtude   32
29. Listing: An alternative vs THE Alternative   33
30. PTSD and PTGD   34
31. White Horse syndrome   35
32. Obstinacy: Some people & cultures cannot change
    their minds   36
33. Force multipliers   37
34. Constant judgements   38
35. Depolarize   39
36. Professional revenge   40
37. Domains of Competence   41
38. The Hub   42
39. Optimal deprivation   43
40. Un-happiness   44
41. On losing more   45
42. Speak to my need, not off your script   46
43. Hidden hierarchies   47
44. Look to see   48
45. Choice words   49
46. Businessman as an athlete?   50
47. Wisdom of old people   51
48. Early on the brakes in trouble, hard on the gas in
    good times   52
49. The suitcase carousel question   53
50. Mental Toughness test   54
51. Framing a prejudice first before the other party does   55
52. Collective illusions   56
53. Light but Fast   57
54. 'Strategy without tactics is the slowest way to victory'
    – Sun Tzu   58
55. Big-itis   59
56. Small-itis   60
57. Agreement precision   61
58. Intelligence and Integrity   62

59.	Indirect warfare	63
60.	Pressure	64
61.	Peloton	65
62.	Who has proved you wrong?	66
63.	Incrementals	67
64.	Runes and Reputations	68
65.	The Hero's Journey	69
66.	If you want to train a good longbowman, start with his grandfather	70
67.	Changing the gait	71
68.	Command or control?	72
69.	Nested identities	73
70.	'What are you really capable of?'	74
71.	Un-solveables	75
72.	Information vs conclusion	76
73.	Likeability + competence matrix	77
74.	Competitive types are disagreeable	78
75.	Process or Outcome? West or East?	79
76.	The Optimists dilemma: betting against your belief	80
77.	Discipline vs creativity	81
78.	Find hungry samurai	82
79.	Armor yourself with an image	83
80.	Not you but the task	86
81.	Regroup	87
82.	You can only appeal to what's right or wrong; or to consequences	88
83.	Rite of passage	89
84.	Pleasure peaks	90

INTRODUCTION

The lessons of the first 4 volumes of Unconventional CEO were very illuminating to me. The reaction of readers and colleagues made a case for this additional offering. It is satisfying to flesh out ideas that found themselves in notebooks, often dated years ago. At times new insights pop up from seeing the machinery of business buzz in action.

There is no particular order to this book. Start at any page. Pick it up and read at random. Make critical notes and add your own insights. Disagree, object, change it for the better. Take time to measure the contents against your own experience. You may finds that you probably know every idea. None came from the text books; these are lessons learned and ideas taken from the hard knocks school. There should be a thread of plain and un-common sense running through it all – with some twists and kinks.

My hope is that you enjoy and pass it on.

Mario Pretorius
Bakoven, Cape Town, 2023

Author's Biography

I spent a lifetime riding my luck, my Viking hammingja, and it is liberating to be able to share some of the ideas and practises that I learned the unconventional and more often, the hard way.

I have spent a lifetime preparing for things that may never happen; the peaceful revolutions and the earth-shattering theories. On the way, I picked up an MBA from the Graduate School of Business (GSB) in Cape Town and attended some postgraduate courses there, as well as at Harvard Business School. My working experience includes multiple-year stints in Oslo, Milwaukee, Toledo and Ann Arbor, Michigan.

My corporate life included the very large (South African Breweries), the large (Malbak Subsidiaries) and the medium. I have listed three companies on the Johannesburg Securities Exchange (JSE Ltd). Because, but mostly in spite of, my best efforts, I have succeeded in business in multiple disciplines as founder and owner across various industries, from property development to telecommunications.

Through the Junior Chamber of Commerce I visited many countries, made lifelong friends and acquired an appetite for learning and understanding. After I fired myself as CEO of TeleMasters into the Chairmanship, I hoped a restless soul would settle. Forays into multiple-country farming, marine diamond mining, (more) property development, data centre building and a child-feeding programme means there is some life left in the (older) dog. Not sure what is next, but there are half a dozen ideas in the nursery.

My full bio is on LinkedIn and on Who's Who. You can follow me on Twitter here: @unconCEO. My website is www.MarioPretorius.co.za. Please feel free to contact me.

DEDICATION

Perhaps this is my last effort to put ideas to paper – the one's not found in management books. I keep learning and revisiting the ways we did business before – and will in the future. Rubbing shoulders with the Great and the Good is always a privilege; I dedicate these pages to those who stimulated my thoughts, shared lessons and experiences that stimulated conversation, debate and some ideas that made it to these pages.

I am grateful to the new acquaintances I have made and to the many good criticisms of the unconventional; else it wouldn't be fun!

Dear CEO

Few would ever know the weight that Atlas carries. Did you know that corporate excellence was your destiny? The thought of the sword of Damocles would never pierce their happy dreams. You, however, chose a different path and gazing down from the pinnacle, may ask; 'How do I best stay here for a while?" Your hard work is paying off, your acuity in seeing things that work and making them your own is rewarding you.

A lifetime of learning and dedication to your craft moulded you to sit at the head of the Boardroom table. Perhaps you got here by an unconventional route, then these pages are meant for you. If not, perhaps you can add some arrows to your quiver too – enjoy the read. It's common sense in different words; make it your own and start writing your own Manual soon.

1.

RECONSTITUTED PIRATES

The history of 'business' is not a pretty tale. Wars and piracy supported the rise of nations, as did raids, slavery, stripping of natural resources, theft of conquered land and the riches of vanquished peoples. Colonialism, missionary work and invasive immigration was aided by trade barriers, duties, tolls as well as coercive and monopolistic practices.

What we have today is the genteelest version of a supposed borderless and integrated free-trade economy, relatively honest and profitable. It is a world far removed from its history and the human spirit is not benevolent unless bored, rich or cowed and innocent. Those with deep lines at the corners of the eyes have seen far shores and the heart of darkness.

These old crusties are a scarcity at the helm nowadays; captains of industry rarely venture beyond the plush and have no idea or appetite for the dog watch in the teeth of the roaring twenties. It used to be that risk and reward peaked at many multiples; a single successful journey to the Spice Islands would mean a pensionable fortune – else death. Flipping Contracts For Difference is the closest to risk and tremors that the modern C-suite comes to a big win or lose.

Somewhere there's a button to release the Captain Jack in you onto the High Seas of Privateering for glory. Find it and control him, you are a reconstituted buccaneer after all – and still leery of paying tribute and taxes.

2.

THE HARD YARDS

Not everyone can do them – or will want to. This is the ultimate test of competence and only a few will pass. The hard yards is that distance to get things finally done, no matter what the obstacles are. It is a *lebensanschau* with all the extra gears beyond first. It is seen when someone does whatever it takes to get something done; to solve the intractable or make something good from a hopeless situation. A remarkably few wear the Victoria Cross or similar and are thinly scattered amongst all ranks.

Surely you've been in such a situation and display those chest ribbons in your mind's eye? It's not only the yards, but it's the' hard' part that is essential here – who will routinely go beyond expectations to tame the impossible? Wesley in stores does that; he finds the unfound, restructures the impossible mess and is a solid player under all circumstances – a real man from la Mancha. In contrast Pete will close that difficult deal – almost, but not quite.

There's just something he cannot wrestle down, he's short on the yards and only the easy stuff stays within reach. Like a cornered leopard or a cowed pup? – who has that instinct to persevere and innovate until the task is done, the winning try scored or the enemy Legion standard captured notwithstanding all the salty bodily fluids expended? Hoops of steel are what you need to tie these Yarders to your soul with and only if you can be a brother to them in the same way. The world requires bravery for victory. Few can answer that call. Find the Wesley's and keep them close at hand.

> *"Out of every one hundred men, ten shouldn't even be there, eighty are just targets, nine are the real fighters, and we are lucky to have them, for they make the battle. Ah, but the one, one is a warrior, and he will bring the others back."* – Heraclitus

3.

CAN YOU AFFORD YOUR EMPLOYEES?

Not so fast – compensation is only part of the affordability package you negotiated with the mercenaries (they're there for the money, right?).

You are invested far deeper than that. Can you afford the time spent with that person? Can you afford the emotionality that flows from these interactions – if it's negative? Can you afford the effects of concerns and worries about the correct and agreed achievements? Can you afford the allocation of other people's time to guide or correct errant outcomes?

The 'affordability' should be clear: you have a very, very limited capacity beyond coinage to 'spend' on each person under direct command and even less to those further down the line. It's not only a cost to your time but also to that most precious of all your attributes that is affected: positive energy.

Frustration, misunderstanding and conflict all tap that reservoir needlessly. Avoiding the issues is merely postponement and comes with usury. David is such a Board member, Eben is that manager. It is time to set them free. Their contributions are great but unaffordable. There are surely someone else less dear and more endearing?

4.

STORY TELLING

When your lips move, people around you stop and listen. Not only to calculate a response, but to hear, understand and remember. That's why you should tell your ideas and comments as stories as often as you can – these should be uninterruptible, memorable and enjoyable. You will have to get good – very, very good at this else it's yabba-dabba as before but only in an irritating way.

Few know the often horrid lessons that lurk behind our favourite fairy tales; how the Princess smashed the frog against the wall after it retrieved her golden ball; Red Riding Hood is a coming of age metaphor and the cheating of Rumpelstiltskin of his due. Aspiring to this level on mastery on an hourly basis is perhaps ambitious but hone your skills until you can make a Charlie Munger smile.

Can you tell a joke and get genuine laughter? Good start – can you do a running commentary that has everyone in stiches? The tools of brevity, wit and the unexpected endings is your recipe – and then you better practise. Stories must grab attention and have the audience identify with the good protagonist. End with all accepting the jesting outcome as a gentle but firm reminder of what was expected but perhaps not delivered.

Stories form a camaraderie and your spell-weaving keeps the distress levels down when everyone knows there's a lesson or a guidance coming. Lower tension is conducive to listening and the day that you smile fades is when the frost sets and harder words will be spoken, softly. It might not be your accountant nature – but remember you didn't lecture your own toddlers, you gained their trust and storied them to co-operation and learning. There are many missives to be delivered, make each one memorable while carving your Leader Totem Pole. Make them hang … on your lips.

5.

HORMESIS

In small quantities some poisons could be beneficial and stimulate the start of repair mechanisms. That's what low dose radiation can do, activating that which is not activated in its absence. This is hormesis. Stupidity also falls in this category albeit in micro doses.

This means that there can be unique benefit in low exposure of a dangerous substance. Perhaps some ions of your nuclear wrath when stupidity triumphs can be hormetic as fallout to the spectators and those who hid in the bunkers.

The radioactive glow should activate and strengthen their resolve to do the right things right. Exposure to this rare gamma could grow a stronger specimen, in contrast to those who were incinerated at ground zero. In further contrast, nothing should radiate upwards to you from other confrontations. Keep the danger levels low to get hormesis and not horrors.

6.

CLEAR RISKS

As an Unconventional, you might have studied Risk Theory. Perhaps you believed Black-Scholes to be true (spoiler – it isn't). Many fancy and complicated theories abound, a few can be pulled out of your pocket in an instant to display. Greater minds than ours have common sense truths like 'don't bet big to win small'.

Perhaps more pennies may drop on understanding clear risk. Primary to the 'no risk gets no reward' axiom is that some are willing to take more risk. Some others even play risk at an eye-watering level.

Our frontal cortex only matures at 25 and until that hallowed day the Darwin Awards have many candidates-in-waiting. There is no end to the stupidity of youngsters. Some of them clock in at your ship too. Penny two: The young are dangerous and tolerance of failure is a prerequisite for accolades. That applies to them and also to you.

You might sit on your hands, he might lose his ass on the downside of that bet. Keep the risks you take isolated from fallout to the other below decks. Fail better, overcome and repeat. This leads to the third penny: clear risks are preferable to unknown risks.

Your grunts may go a long way for you, and even further if their risks are clarified. Same applies to your vision of tomorrow: the better the risks are detailed, the more extensive the remedies and recoveries can be prepared. The third use of a walking stick after uphill walking aid and fighting off wolves is to determine the depth of the stream to cross. Tolerate known risk but probe the unknown first. Never leave base without your staff in hand and a clear idea of what is expected ahead.

7.

IS RISK-TAKING A BUG?

Life is sometimes stranger than fantasy. We assume we're each born with a certain fixed propensity for taking risks to gain reward. *Toxoplasma gondii* has different ideas. This protozoa infects felines and a fair number of their owners where it permanently migrates to the brain to settle. It had its secrets discovered only recently and *Toxo* gets riskless rewards. From time to time it feels like multiplying sexually and has its eggs passed via cat faeces to a nibbling rodent.

Such an infected rodent finds cat urine a sexual stimulant and hunts down that cat. It offers its trembling body to be eaten, passing on the *Toxo* eggs in its brain to a new owner and a new cycle. Were there risk or reward for the cat?

A recent study found a pack of Yellowstone wolves were found to be partially infected by *T. gondii*.

Here is where *Toxo* sprang its magic: infected wolved were 46 times more likely to fight for and win leadership in the pack and the loser were 11 times more likely to leave the pack and form their own. This is a jarring number; the infected wolves lost all sense of fear and failure, it was win or leave to a degree that is magnificently incomprehensible to Naturalists. While science watched the rat victim, the wolf carrier went scientifically off the charts.

Estimates are that half of the world's humans carry *Toxo* – and are such wolves in waiting – or are they? No definitive studies have yet been done on cat lovers' tendency to take over the planet, but that Bond nemesis, Stavros Blofeld and his lap kitty comes to mind. Would you volunteer for such a biological *neuralink* that could guarantees a successful leadership outcome?

https://www.sciencenews.org/article/wolves-parasite-pack-leader-toxoplasma-gondii

There is a downside. Infected males showed lower superego strength (rule consciousness), higher vigilance, were more likely to disregard rules and were more expedient, suspicious, jealous, and dogmatic. Hardly standard leader material. Lady carriers showed higher warmth and higher superego strength and were more warm hearted, outgoing, conscientious, persistent, and moralistic. Does this mean better leadership and mothering skills?

The infected males had a significantly higher testosterone level and this begs the question – bugs or drugs for high-T thugs?

https://www.ncbi.nlm.nih.gov/pmc/articles/PMC2526142/

8.

HONESTY SETTINGS

Do we have fixed 'settings' for our principles and reactions? Are these the same for all situations? Obviously there are gradations that we're aware of; humour is toned down in tragic settings and guilt fluctuates by our mental state. What would the ideal setting be, for example, of 'honesty'? Are yours at 90% at work, 70% for your kids (you have to tell them that they're the best in the world) or back to 99% with your buds between brews?

It is worthwhile listing the attributes that are changeable and consciously determining your setting thereof. Here's an example: Honesty in business: 90%. No self-incrimination. No false answers ever – silence or avoidance. No soul destroying take-down of behaviour. No explanations if the reasons would be confusing. No breaking secrets. Avoidance of knowing others' secrets. No stealing of company or people resources – including time. The missing 10% – dishonesty – is probably used for marketing and tax matters?

It follows that unsuitable people need to be let go as soon as possible in order not to steal their progress somewhere elsewhere more fitting of their 'setting' profile; whether higher (painful) or lower (even more painful).

Why not a 100% setting? That would be top of the Autism scale: brutal and tone-deaf. This makes one wonder about the concept of honesty and truth and also the scale and subtleties thereof. Should you scale up or down over time or circumstances? Firmly NO. Decide on what you would and would not tolerate. Engrave that on your professional soul and state it. Do this with all those around you, detail and note down what the 'loose' percentage means and what the consequences are. Expand to your empire of like-minded settlers.

What other setting come to mind? Empathy? Compromise and tolerance? Know thyself and confirm thy choices.

9.

WHAT IS 'FUNDAMENTAL' TO YOUR ORGANIZATION?

A 'fundamental' is the origin, the primary source on which most of the objectives, strategies, goals and measurables are based on. This is a textbook mouthful.

Like Shakespeare to literature, this fundamental premise defines the forthcoming expectations and actions. It will define your management and leadership outlook as well. What will you choose? Profit? Cash? Long employment? ESG? Perhaps another metric that you have convinced your Board to be the primary pursuit of the assembled assets and talent under your whip?

This choice of 'fundamental' warrants a careful analysis and delicate choices. You cannot afford a soggy philosophy here. It must be crisp, inspiring and executable. From this 'fundamental' your Hussars will focus their labours and you will want to reward them for doing so. The 'mission' and 'vision' fads did an injustice to clear thinking and a clear definition on how success will be measured. Whatever you choose as fundamental will have to give docking space for the more mundane expectations of the owner's and their chosen representatives.

Assume you decide that 'domination of the cloud based disaster recovery of data centre clients' is where you want to plant the flag. What would be the fundamental issue needed to achieve this? The outcome must be profitable, but how much and when? Cash needs to flow – which direction and how often? Expertise must be employed and deployed – in what way and tendered by who?

These pesky items are under your control and need to support the fundamental issue. Perhaps you defined it so narrow as 'continuous reduction of safety-issue downtime in underground mining' i.e. like my entity SperoSens Instruments or as wide as 'an ecosystem of mutual supportive technologies to define the future of the human race' -i.e. Tesla. Either way, products and services, installation, support and every other strategy and decision should and indeed must be measured against this fundamental.

10.

NATURE IS CHAOS

Chaos is good. The one opposite of chaos is a sterile order. Nature is fundamentally chaotic – in an orderly way. The other opposite of chaos is disaster, where chaos escaped order. Healthy cells multiply in your body at random times; if not random, your body will end up lumpy. If not orderly, it will be cancer.

Winds blow, sunspots attempt to fry the earth, earthquakes shake and poles flip. In the man-made world traffic congests and stock prices move almost randomly. On short timelines even human nature seems disastrously wedged between four Apocalyptic horsemen. Still here we are in the 130th century since the taming of wheat in Sumer region and now we have accessible AI.

Capitalism is ongoing chaotic competition. So too are Democracy and politics. The 'short term orderly world' is less successful – central planning, socialism, utopias and section title property. The later your career peaks the higher your probability of successfully having navigated a chaotic life in a chaotic world. Taming chaos is a better strategy than fighting it.

Chaos will endure locally until our Sun flips to a class A-1 Supernova – literally in the blink of an eye. By then the orderly chaos will be only on a much, much larger scale until its explosion as a black hole into neutrinos.

Embrace your chaos and direct its process of ripping up order. Entropy awaits all but the process to get there is the rollercoaster of life. Find yourself a front seat with some popcorn.

11.

REPLACEMENT THEORY

Improve or destroy? At the crossroads of mediocrity and disaster, there is a need for drastic change. Product flared out? Campaign bombed or frontline failed? There is a choice is between redoing better with what you have at hand or chucking out all and replacing it with the new.

Some argue for the middle ground but that could only bring intermediate relief. The unconventional argument is to start over in the wisdom of the Alcoholics Anonymous' definition of insanity; repeating that which didn't work before but expecting a different outcome.

Many leaders are panel beaters at heart when they should rather walk away from the wreck. Not wanting to waste a broken resource with the time, effort and cost of a backward looking introspection? Start anew and jettison the vestiges of failure, people and all.

The unconventional message is clear: success has the rewards everyone is looking for and the alternative in failure is not sympathy but sacrifice. Replacement theory is cruel to be kind; keep the smell of lingering disaster away from your winners.

12.

MOTIVATION RESTS ON THE ABILITY TO ENDURE

The brain will trick the body into giving up before the last ounce of effort is expended. It will also trick your stressed endocrine system into preservation mode; more sleep, less activity with its consequences. The road to greatness is often over the horizon and that is not well paved.

When ability meets the enduring will to win there is an ongoing and ever-increasing probability of success. The hard part is enduring the many, varied and relentless hinderances on the way there. Lesser men may question the pace or the price; for you the ability to continuously endure will set you apart.

In sporting life, it's the spirit that functions independently of logical and sane limitations. Better outcomes rely on doing more undo-able's. The universe is merely testing you – someone will get the prize and its earned by sweat, ulcers and often the miserable loneliness of having no-one to ask for the answers of a grim and tiring reality.

Dig deep and dig often. That's the way to find treasure. Don't stop digging, don't stop innovating and don't stop for the pain. Endurance creates its own motivation – you didn't fight for what you want only to fall short of the glory. Practise to endure not only the blows of misfortune but also the delay in good fortune. *Vasbyt.*

13.

NCO vs Officers

War business is analogous to real business in some ways. The staffing is perhaps only partially so as most employees are expected to return intact from being sent out to confront a hostile world. The structure of the Command of Officer and Under officer and infantry have undergone many adaptations since ancient times.

From Roman Commander to Legionnaire, the command was dispersed through 7 levels. Last century German military training, would-be officers had to secure the unanimous vote of the regiment's Officers to advance. What is interesting and topical, is how the 'mules' of the military, the Non-Commissioned Officers are structured and deployed.

In most military set-ups, Officer's razor sharp minds are deployed in strategy and tactic formulation whilst the NCO corps execute these through actions in the lower ranks. In the Russian military, the Officers interact directly with the front line. This increases the pressure of operational urgency over tactical importance on the Officer. It also decreases the ability of the soldier to step up, cover a wide chasm, to wearing epaulettes.

Is this story and distinction important? In today's 'flat structure' so beloved by the management consultants it has a distinct drawback in the faster moving organization. You may be grinding down the sharpness in lower ranks by menialities instead of fostering 'NCO's' to learn by doing while being groomed for the upper ranks.

Your organization is probably hierarchical. Organizational flatness has great benefits in terms of flexibility of deployment and costs. Still, home-grown management is a more enduring option than replenishing your talent pool by outsiders. You need a 'NCO' structure to transit your best talent to wearing stars.

14.

CROSS-SELLING AND OTHER FANTASIES

There is a terror in drawing a grid of all clients and with all products on offer. Inevitably it is filled as a meagre and spotty picture of seemingly lost or beckoning opportunities. Why can't we sell all our product to existing and loyal clients? Plans are then drawn up and after lots of finger-wagging at the salespeople kicks off the downhill rush to Nirvana as the hushed onlookers wait. Then wait some more. Why aren't the orderbooks exploding?

Dream on. Hardly any clients use your full range of products. However 'loyal' they are, they might still be rational in their own unique way and your offerings range may be only a fraction of their total requirements. It is obviously more profitable to sell more to the existing crowd. Somehow it is also more difficult too, perhaps due to the human propensity for risk mitigation by diversification. The spread amongst many suppliers is an instinctive reaction. Your own list of suppliers will confirm that.

What about obtaining references? Or referrals? Or obtaining exclusivity? Scheduled interactions with yourself to deepen the bonds? Why are these logical actions so resisted by clients? It is said that when in an intimate social setting that if you still have to ask, you won't get. There is a rhythm of interaction in the sales relationship between vendor and buyer. Choices are made, rationalised, hardened and protected. A new sale needs to tick all these boxes – with a jaded partner.

It may work when offering a second or third product but often the magic lacks notwithstanding the irrefutable benefit and logic it is offered with. People need variety and Buyers are people too.

15.

KNOWING ABOUT VS. UNDERSTANDING

The classic conundrum of width of knowledge vs. depth of understanding is rather common. A betting man would lay odds that few employees really understand their own aspiration, how the job at hand fits into the mechanism of organisation, why things are done this way or even where it all leads to.

Case in point: the CEO knows how depreciation is calculated but does he fathom the IRFRS audit rules that govern it? Or the Rockwell hardness for the widget alloy? Does knowing these things matter? The Antikythera mechanism exquisitely told time, tides, moon and star movements so that the seafarer knew what seas to expect. It is doubtful that the ship's Captain understood that 276 geared teeth were needed to move the Saturn orbit.

The Unconventional top-dog needs to carefully list the things he needs to understand. First of all is figure out the interconnectedness of the gears and the points of possible disastrous failure thereof. Understanding means seeing the planets' orbits move as expected. Knowing where they should move to makes you an observer, understanding how to get them fixed if they don't makes you a wizard.

Hopefully your corporate automaton ticks over relentlessly accurate. Knowing where to dab the oil keeps it that way. Specialization of your line functionaries may preclude them from seeing the entire universe of the enterprise. That's where your guidance in meetings should illuminate the totality. Ask the person in the spotlight to explain their specialist view in depth to his peers. This may elicit both added perspective and admiration.

That's how you learn, too. To boost the personal aspirations of the daily faithful, reveal their irreplaceability and help them see the Lifetime Value of their earnings in your team. Surely they would understand that.

16.

Keep away from Absolutism at the edges

It is easier to take and extreme position than to carefully think through a situation and offer a nuanced stand. It's also more emotionally satisfying to choose a high castle on the bank whence to fight from than wading the unknown river. Extreme positions and absolutes are more defensive than helpful to gain understanding.

When facing a new challenge, you may find yourself among the extremophiles in a white-or-black situation. Either they're for the invasion or dead-set against it. Sounds like successful propaganda either way, right? Are things so clear cut in general? How can you find the position that is advantageous between the extremes?

You need to think this through before putting up a marker. This does not imply straddling or sitting the fence but you must state a clear position based on your interpretation of relevant facts. Put your idea into play and encourage a vigorous debate. Flying off the handle, jumping to conclusions and other exercises may lead to injury or embarrassment, yours is a definitive voice and it does not need praise or support to be correct.

17.

SET THE FRAME BEFORE YOU LAUNCH INTO A TOPIC

Attentive listeners can soak up more of your ideas and wisdom than mere casual ears. This sounds logical. Unless you've set the stage for them to listen, they might only hear – while formulating a reply back as soon as you shut up. Your listener must have context to place and evaluate your idea or comment. Require the same framing from other speakers.

Shooting off on a topic without sketching the background tor context is an incomplete story. High-IQ individuals like you and your ilk may have rapid answers to ordinary questions – and unless set in situ, your answer may cover a different question altogether. Once every ear is up to speed, the conversation will make more sense, all around.

A very brief introduction and situational description (in short) will set the scene where your heroics or wisdom-reflecting answers can be shown off uniquely. Practice this and get the habit ingrained in your audience too. They might now listen to learn.

18.

MOVING TARGETS OF RETURN

Business is not static, not even for a moment. Yet the expectations of outcomes are often graven in stone tablets as if they were Laws – and these need to be shattered too. Sales turnover, margins achieved, operational cash churned out are never the same from day to day. Some mystical statistic deems there would be swings & roundabouts to get to the exact magic forecasted numbers. This won't happen.

This dynamic of fixed targets and outcomes produces ulcers and despair. The aberrations of a fickle clientele can drive managers and CEO's to drastic and often irresponsible actions just to meet the numbers. The 'month' is maybe too long a time to judge the ebb and tide of the client response. The dipping of management toes into the cold water of reported figures should be anticipated by frequent report-backs, not dreaded at the formal results meetings.

Similarly, in a business with more than one division, market or product, the outcomes will surely vary from period to period. Iron-clad expectations should be revisited and adapted with frequency. This is not to condone underperformance, but to imbue the organization players with great realism.

Downgrading the likelihood of success early also means that the resources and scarce managerial attention will be directed elsewhere, perhaps permanently. So the flogging over poor reported numbers must cease and a funeral could be called for if the prospects wither. Life moves on and business is unforgiving in its progress.

What gave 83% return this year may become unexpected and unrealistic in future. The 15% target expected, unmet, should not have been a surprise but the remedial action should have been implemented before the outcomes presentation. Farming returns were good last quarter, trading too but the BTC price was poor. What are the prospects and where should we focus? Results are backward looking, forecasts are linear. Best amend early – with con-sequences.

Expect changing fortunes and markets, slow successes and quick disappointments. It follows that the overheads and fixed cost should be flexible else the concrete may harden around your shoes on the pier.

19.

CHANGING THE PAST

Would you want the ability to go back in time and change the past to influence the present?

You know that's impossible, or is it? Today is tomorrow's past. It's up to you to change tomorrow. That's the way to make as sure as possible that you are changing the past to something you don't yearn to redo differently later.

Champagne after harvest time flows from good planting and from those hundreds of small things done well that makes a good farmer. Don't miss out a single step, nature is unforgiving. Business is a war that may play out even worse after neglect. Share this with your comrades-in-arms.

20.

SURVIVE-ABILITY NOT SUSTAINABILITY

The hollow words of the politically correct and their baggage drivers through the management landscape are at best an irritation if not an affront to sensibility. The whole 'sustainability' idea of an operational business as a goal is a non-starter; 'sustainability' is used as if keeping the business going as long as possible and then planning an end game is a brand-new concept.

When is a business sustainable – when it lasts 10 years? Or 20? How can mining be sustainable on a dwindling resource? If a farmer improves the soil quality for better yields – is that sustainable or actually growth?

Let's try survive-ability – doing smart things and refrain from dumb things to make sure tomorrow won't see the doors getting shuttered. Beyond survival lies modest growth and the continuous search for opportunity to add the new and the better. Best to use word of which the implications are known, understood and remembered.

Business requires precise language for detailed instructions. Woolly terms and vague meanings have no place; nonsense word like 'curate' and the like should carry consequences for its user.

21.

The need for plane crashes

Lifting weights stresses those muscles and the pleasant result is getting ripped and looking good. The outcome depends on whether it is done correctly and the science, art and experience of physical improvement precedes even the Minoan culture. Still most practitioners stay amateurs with mediocre improvement as they attempt the shortcut of improvisation.

Understanding the combinations of time, effort, nutrition, sleep and correct method application and then undertaking the journey of hard slog and dedication may bring ego-stroking satisfaction. Pushing iron is relatively low risk and one should get perfectly good at its basics. Watching standard gym people unfortunately shows very little mastery despite all the paid Professional Trainers' efforts.

An aircraft disaster is a much better example of learning. Every plane crash makes flying thereafter safer. It is a tragedy to lose lives and equipment but ameliorated by the system that gets to understand the reasons in events of doom. After investigation, legal requirements for future prevention are considered and air travel becomes less risky. Pilots must get perfectly good at the basics. They learn to get better.

Some systems in your operation can do with muscling up but others may be critical in need of attention to be fail-safe. Is there a robust process that dissects each failure and the near-misses with an implementable set of improvements to follow? Would you be able to ask 'switch off the power to the IT room and have all equipment and processes fired up without data loss in 15 minutes'? What happens when laptops get stolen? If the CRM system goes wonky? CFO arrested for DIU? Supplier goes bust? Bank recalls loans?

Beyond your plan 'B's, these situations must be returned to normal – unless there is a better normal to move to. Prevent the crashes and learn from others' failures and harden your responses.

22.

MAKE IT, DON'T LOOK FOR IT

Easier said … Yes, few can build a house from scratch, yet it can be done. The 17 or so skills need can be learned or delegated. Planning can be outsourced. There was no limitation to time or help in the first sentence above. Adding skill mean that the context of its application can be understood.

Things and applications can be made if it isn't available. Your supervisors should buy in on this by skilling up their people. More skills means versatility and redundancy at overlaps. Good skills lead to enhancing the secret sauce of success. Should a certain thing be made if it cannot be found? Maybe not, but if it could be, your depth of resources just increased. Morale and confidence climbs higher. Such commitment means that your U-boat can make repairs else give up the fight for a return to port. With that insight comes the preparation of what's needed and who's needed for the mission.

The constant culling and replacement of specialists on your watch is the best indicator of successful execution. 'What game to play with what tactics' quickly becomes 'who must we select to win at it.' Your job is almost halfway done once your crew are ready to make it happen themselves.

23.

LEARN TO SERVE FIRST

Let's get all mushy here. To serve comes from the base word *weoch* – 'workship' – mistranslated from Akkadian in all modern Bibles as 'worship'. In democracy we elect those who will serve the community. In politics, the elected often regard themselves as the 'leaders'; a complete turnaround of the intent. Thus they lord over the rest of us in splendour and blue-light brigades, almost untouchable and definitely uncontactable until the next round of idle promises are rolled out pre-election.

Even if you are the sole proprietor, you are not the only person involved in the success of the enterprise. Customers have to be served and so too does the management and the foot soldiers. Even Generals that stave off the Barbarians. What do they require – all of them?

This is where the CEO serves. His responsibilities are arrows, shelter, division of loot and a safe passage home. He needs to serve before requiring service.

There is a wider community out there. Perhaps you can extend your altruism to the Junior Chamber, Round Table, Kiwani's and other community organizations who serve others without requiring reciprocity, even if it's just for the feeling of building communities with the things money cannot readily buy.

Two decades of my life was spent volunteering in different service organizations, transforming lives that solidified some abilities to find the itches to scratch around me before the troops got too restless. There is much to be gleaned from and given to non-competing people with deep minds and open hearts. Find them in their groups and join up for a stint.

24.

TEST FOR CHARACTER BY ASKING FOR UNREHEARSED RESPONSES

Your Lieutenants are more than just the personas that make rain for the shareholders. One third of their weekdays and most of their past shape their motivations, approaches, comfort zones and hot-buttons. Learn about these features of each one in a case-study way. Describe a hypothetical situation to then pop the question 'what would you do?' An example: Tesla faces a Lithium shortage.

You want to observe the 'why' of the answers, their proposed outcome is just a talking point. You would be looking for depth of understanding, and an ability to generate options, flexibility in adapting if circumstances change. You expect confirmation of your opinions of their abilities and character. Your responses could be tested as well but the wily fox in you will probably project those question on a junior, right?

How did they do? If unspectacular, dissect, discuss, repeat and observe. If clarity in the response of depth of analysis remans absent, you have reason for doubting their career prospects. You're looking at how they respond – the character – and not necessary the cleverness of the answers.

25.

PRICE'S LAW, SQUARE ROOT OF X IS 50%.

The 80/20 rule is the Pareto principle – where the 20% of something causes 80% of the outcomes. The real magic is Price's Law that shows a far more condensed version of outcomes. Price's Law is not new, but reasonably unknown – and understanding it is unconventional.

The principle is that half the outcome is determined by the square root of the participants (in this example).

In all their World Cup Rugby games, the Springboks scored 171 tries. 50% of 171 is **86 tries**, rounded up.

The test for Price's Law is as follows:

161 different Boks played in the 7 World Cups.

The square root of 161 is **13 players** (rounded up)

The 14 highest scoring Boks, from Habana (15 tries) to Schalk Brits (3) scored an accumulated 83 tries

Thus about half the tries was scored by approximately the square of the players.

Close enough for validation

Another example: On the PGA tour 2022:

50 Tournaments, 175 players.

The square root of 175 is **13 players**

In reality just 10 players won 25 tournaments, even tighter than Price's Law of 50%

What is there to learn from this? In your 10-man start-up, 3 people will accomplish 50% of outcomes (square root of 10). When you pop the corks for the 100th newbie, only 10 people will actually do the 50% (square root of 100).

This has some Tesla-esque implications in staffing efficiency; committee formation, Board composition, team selection and all kinds of general expectations when empire builders start strutting.

Smaller is Better if it's efficiency you're after. The outcomes of your product ranges, marketing campaigns end cost-cutting ventures may be so 'Priced' as well. Expect this and embrace it – a pressure cooker to distil the best of the best.

26.

KEANU GAMES

Mr. Reeves says that highly intelligent people sometimes play a mind game. They try to be wrong once in a while. They also practice being wrong more often to reset their egos.

That's a good start and also a good test. Feed your fellow growlers a bit of inaccurate or misinformation and wait for the correction. If there is none forthcoming, keep feeding. There is a scale to this, at some point in time you may realise that they are swallowing without chewing here – and don't know the taste of truth.

Big mistake. When one of them is right on the money with a wagging finger, you can claim 'Keanu' and heap the praises. Keep your front-liners sharp and sceptic. Trust, but verify, smile but furrow the brow; never accept that which you haven't checked and ticked as true either.

27.

GET HIGH RESOLUTION MODEL OF COMPLEX PROBLEMS BEFORE ATTEMPTING ANSWERS

It is not uncommon to solve tough problems, it is a basic requirement of doing business. In the previous 4 Unconventional CEO volumes some distinctions were made between types of problems but a general principle holds true: the more that is known about the situation, the less the chance of an oversight in the solution.

Conventional thinking holds that the WHAT of the problem/situation should be analysed before attempting to formulate answers. Unconventional thinking demands really high resolution dissection of WHY the situation created is a problem, if at all. Perhaps the definition of 'what a problem is' should pre-empt the discussion.

A sharp look at reality might mean that one person's problem is another's ho-hum of mere annoyance. It might be the wrong 'problem conclusion' too. "There's not enough parking spaces for employee cars" already triggers answers in many sharp minds. First-come first-serve rule could mean a parking status symbol and more so if there's no exception for top brass. Was this a real 'problem'?

Inventory overstock seems a problem until the bad sale forecast is fingered or the hard-to-get items highlighted as the upstream irritant. Deep scrutiny may pay back its investment many times over and define the 'problem' statement with workable accuracy – and only if it is really is a 'problem'.

The more complex the situation seems, the better the chance of finding hidden treasure under an acute gaze of WHY. This is one instance where the blame game can work, like musical chairs. The last one to forego scrutiny might be the one with the real problem. Keep going upstream and sideways for better resolution of the resolution!

28.

NON-SIMILTUDE

Do problems grow exponentially? Could they? Engineering embraces similtude. One model can be scaled up using the same parameters. The moment an extra parameter is added it's not the same case anymore.

Area grows at the square of linear length, but volume and mass grow at the cube of length. A longer fuselage on the plane design will weigh more – a lot more, in fact the cubed lot more. This is *non-similtude*.

This is when things don't scale linear – a pyramid's base is a closer approximation to a hierarchical organisation's people expansion. Growing sales will add people – and lots of them as the needs of increased execution ripple throughout the existing ranks.

Problems somehow seem to be secretly interconnected. Once a nerve is prodded, the rest of its links rise up rebelliously. It's good to stir hard once in a while and get all that simmers to float in full view. The size of the eventual tsunami might well be subject to the concept of non-similtude, a far larger than expected outcome.

Your CFO failing a deadline? Scratch around and the network dysfunction and car allowance unhappiness might growl at you too. Your staff knows that without problems to solve they would not be needed. Issues often look similar or smaller on the surface than what's hidden underneath. They often are different or far larger. The complexities vary. An analysis of the total cost of internal financial services and audits may well unravel from an expected 1% of turnover cost to a 5% hydra-headed systems squid that is fuelled by IFRS demands way beyond your expectations.

Like a good dermatologist, put the patient under the bright lights and look for the unwarranted moles -and strike quickly.

29.

Listing: An alternative vs THE Alternative

Lazy thinking can lull your voyage into the quiet doldrums. Too often the effort and process of thinking through decisions is stopped at the edge of the known; the best available alternative is dressed up as a sacrifice to the god of profit.

Your chilling challenge should be whether an alternative is THE best alternative? What others possible outcomes were probed and found wanting? What crazy and unconventional ideas were considered and why were these cast aside? How many alternatives would be adequate? You want to see the list.

More lists mean the charioteers are applying their minds. No options must be left unconsidered and then no ideas should be left unexplored to fall into other greedy hands later. This listing is hard and exhausting, how else can you explore the future if your choices are all repeated decisions of yore?

The past stagnates brains as well as the flow of new business. Car model change unless you settle for a Morgan. Your models should be updated and re-imagined to entice and perform. It is safe to step on the brakes instead of the accelerator, but the safest place around is in a prison, orange jump-suits shouldn't suit your tribe.

30.

PTSD AND PTGD

Stress can be a killer. Stress is also the first step in growth. How do muscles get bigger, how does the a disaster become a lesson? Induced stress. There should be 'growth' after trauma and plenty of either means a resilient and well-exercised organism.

PTGD is the Post Traumatic Growth **Drive**, the expected reaction of the daily tribulations that must improve the responses of those affected. It differs from the PTSD's 'stress' with a positive slant. Should PTGD miss some, you would know where the next axe should fall.

You don't want just continuation of good but the active search for the better. How could anyone demand improved prospects and medals if they don't show the scars of new battles won? No place for seat-warmers on your bus, only lusty axe-swingers that take their battle songs to the den of the dragon. Whence the self-esteem if not earned under the gaze of the brothers standing shoulder to shoulder? The splattered blood should drip on the CV's where their achievements can be chronicled. From stress to growth – keep the tension high and working in your favour.

31.

White Horse syndrome

The White Horse Syndrome must be stamped out. Those ideas where a hero on this colour steeds arrives to save all are dangerous. A little fantasy about the wonders of the future is healthy. When the future is all expected sweetness and light and where everyone escapes the gingerbread cottage is not.

Many all-positive think gurus preach the absence of the negative and often reality is sacrificed as a counterweight. These Whitehorses see only possibilities without threats – a touch of the politician perhaps? Lala land is for those blowing only 3 candles on their special day.

The downside and the unintended consequences of WHS thinking make ventures uncertain. These outcomes are often only overcome with luck and grit after encircling the unwary and unplanned. Chase up the visions but put their feet to the fire to gauge probabilities. Trust but verify; accept but test – and your starry eyed must swallow enough doses of reality to see the intrusion of the real world too.

32.

OBSTINACY: SOME PEOPLE & CULTURES CANNOT CHANGE THEIR MINDS

Only the minority of businesspeople operate in cultures with an ethos that tolerate and encourage change for improvement. In these situations, making a new decision doesn't carry the stigma of having been wrong in the previous decision, it means progress in the scientific method.

Some business cultures require deep explanation for a change of heart. In others the ideology of protecting your ego, saving 'face' and other unhelpful stonewalling habits can become near impossible to circumvent. In a non-British influenced culture, the first impression, idea or viewpoint is often accompanied by the pouring of emotional concrete to set it fast.

Such obstinacy is seen as firmness, reliability even principledness from the opposing vantage point. Your flexibility is ridiculed as wishy-washy, your change of terms are constant lies and exploring options is considered merely a ploy to find weak spots by which to undermine the other party.

Such culture wars are fascinating but exhausting to those who expect compromise and closure. Your own tribe will also have these adherents of the take-no-prisoners school of interaction, hopefully in lesser numbers. The best remedy for cross-border sojourns is to expect this and prepare for trench warfare if your first impression, first offer and primary tactics fail.

33.

FORCE MULTIPLIERS

Local superiority is the giant-killer in business. Dominating a small but vital area will require overwhelming force to displace it and should break the resolve of your intruding opponent. Such domination can be a force multiplier – the effect of the domination adds a disproportional value to the incumbent.

The brave 300 who kept the Persians from Marathon was worth 60,000 Greeks in open battle. The breaking of the Enigma machine's codes was worth several divisions to the Allies as they could manoeuvre forces in real time to where the enemy was planning to go.

Ownership of the fridges in liquor outlets multiplied South African Brewery's force to destroy rival ICB beer in a matter of months. Owning the semiconductor chips ransoms the entire auto manufacturing world-wide. A single, friendly clerk can get your planning applications to the top of the pile and consign your opponents' work to Hades.

What are the weak and weakest points in the industry and does your opponents have a good handle on these? Finding these wormholes to slip in and multiply your ability to dominate that space is the adrenalin rush that makes up for all the other misfires.

34.

CONSTANT JUDGEMENTS

Yes, you do make constant and ongoing judgements of good/bad/ indifferent all day and night on probably everything that happens in your world. So does anyone else. In traffic, on fresh pyjamas, the quality of the Board Pack, every line therein and the attitude of the presenter – all judged.

You cannot help this continuous oscillation between fight, indifference and flight but you can improve your response from judgmental to brilliant. The rule is that evaluations must start and progress from *facts* to *observations* to *conclusions*. It must not run upstream – that would be *prejudice* to *bias confirmation* to *idiocy*.

Best to start discussions in this order as well: do we agree on the FACTS? Moving on to our respective OBSERVATIONS that are supported by the facts, and new facts tested and added where necessary. In finality to CONCLUSION; perhaps by consensus, majority vote or authoritative power but based on facts, perspective by observations and arguments and then the gavel falls; judgment given, but by due and intellectual process.

35.

DEPOLARIZE

Find the middle ground in a polarised situation to break a deadlock. What facts do we all agree on? How easy is it to prove these? Perhaps not a pushover but the bits of consensus are the pegs that the rest of the debate can be stretched over.

Care to repeat someone's argument succinctly until they agree you understand it correctly? Request your opposing view pointer to encapsulate your stance too until you agree that it is accurate and what you meant. The middle ground may only be patches of unstable swamp grass along the edges but agree not to disturb these footholds.

Glaring differences can now be debated and preferably in the manner described above. Much red-hot air singes the ears as people listen to reply instead of for understanding. Divest the emotional attachment to an argument. It is a proposition that should be moulded in debate to perfection from the input of experts.

Allow the other side some of the glory of making their points the crowns on the issue. They need to earn their keep and what better way to show off their brilliance than to shape up the decisions? You need to progress and not score points. The adage is to debate to find out what's right; argument to find out who's wrong.

36.

PROFESSIONAL REVENGE

Ever been taken hostage in your own domain? Been where you get vague answers when the question is clear? Like many CEO's you might be taken in by the apparent wizardry of the Information Technology Brotherhood.

Friend Gordon, a serious IT player on Microsoft's BOA had a mantra of wanting to fire all IT managers for their evil mulish ways of ensconcing their interests from the C-suite. No arguments can be won against this crowd as the answers are technical traps and any attack will be defended with malice.

The interconnectivity of the data world in almost everything makes it the nervous system, the immune system and the digestion system of the business. Woe be any untitled challengers that step into that ring. The Brotherhood knows best and their minds are made up. This is a little exaggeration of course, but personal experience showed me just how deep professional revenge might become when these self-styled geniuses don't get their way with your money on their terms and at your risk.

Engineers are quite different and friendly questioning of their ability and the feasibility of their output can lead to deeper understanding and cool outcomes. Not so with many self-taught wannabe black-hatters that launch their careers from your servers. This is one department where you want to find someone you can trust to guide your ungrasping brain to beneficial conclusions.

37.

DOMAINS OF COMPETENCE

As a CEO you're expected to be competent – everywhere. As an Unconventional you know that you're the glue that hold all the Competent One's together.

An aura once broken reveals a Naked Emperor. Expectations are the auras around you and the same holds true for the other players in your circle. Imagine an Excel column mis-added or a vehicle that went un-serviced and unnoticed so? Perhaps small cracks but it could be indicative of someone not working incessantly on his competency, the way you expect him to.

As a leader you want those auras on display. You should be asking opinions, explanations, context, perspective and interact as often as you can. This will add to your understanding of the complexities of their worlds. Your glue must also contain the fibres of communication, to and from, up and down.

It should look to others as if you're competent all over. You won't have all the answers at hand, but you can get and present them with deep perspectives and with actionable alternatives. The competences of you team should light up your halo and lighten your load.

38.

THE HUB

Are all the important communications from your Commanders channelled through you? Should it be? Are the rules explicit or dependent on situations and personalities? Which levels of information or reporting are excluded?

An easy opt-out would be to require anything *changing* the status quo of a department to be communicated via the Boss – levels to be agreed on. Set, say, certain amounts and timeline deviations. At the other extreme is a requirement for written and distributed daily status reports. Where to best keep your finger on the pulse without blocking the artery?

The art of management drapes around the supposed science thereof and here is where your artistic tendencies must become legend. Like a moving sculpture your actions morph frequently to allow the dissemination of crucial items without drought or overflow. As situations change, you, as the eventual hub must move to remain the centre of command.

Elevate yourself out of the crossflow as much as you can. Like an able fireman you're working on prevention of the infernos and the occasional dousing of red-hot ego's in a blame blaze. Unclutter your hub so that you may better smell smouldering kindling early and see the glow of heated, frenzied actions that show a disaster being remedied before the flames erupt. It used to be called Management by Walking Around; it's now more Management by Listening Very Carefully.

39.

OPTIMAL DEPRIVATION

This might be the best way to raise kids towards independence and an appreciation of objects and experiences. You wouldn't want to raise them in abundance and safety – tied to a bed with a drip and Netflix? Better to fight in order to own instead of to receive freely for no effort; things only have proper value to someone once stained with sweat, blood or tears of frustration.

Deny your underlings the good life until the war is won and the peace seems eternal. Let them earn their spurs, challenge the chains of mediocrity and set them on the enemy with enough rations for a one-way voyage. Else you would be rewarding them too early and will have no space to stoke their hunger for winning.

Who knows what 'optimal' is in every situation? Less is always better as long as 'more' is on offer in the siege. Without an appetite you cannot move the man towards food. Rewards are to be earned and the harder the journey the sweeter the appreciation of success. Do not just feed the hero-in-waiting, that is meant for the condemned man.

40.

UN-HAPPINESS

Abundant propaganda coerces humans to strive to 'be happy'. Smiley face abound and Disney whips up fairy tales from the macabre originals into happy-ever-afters. Except that this is wrong, mistaken and a grievous sin against our existence.

We are built for adventure, not happiness. Our psyche drives an anatomy that sweats when it exercises (only horses do so too), implying we are marathoneers, peaks scalers and crocodile hunters. To rule the earth and lord over lesser men needs more than aloha flower garlands. The call of the wild resonates in our innards, twitches the Achilles tendons in warm-up for conquest and boils the blood for loot and spoils.

THAT is what should get you up before your coffee craving kicks in – the 04:00 ritual of counting skulls and planning for extra storage space for more adventure. Happiness seeking is for the spineless and the weak; those who missed out on the rush to the boats with longswords scything the air.

'Happiness' is a single prune in a world where your banquet reaches the horizon and beyond. Reminisce when fingering the scars, sing war chants with the old crowd now enfeebled by rampage and its aftermath; but never, ever let this sodden, pathetic and destitute word cross your lips again.

41.

ON LOSING MORE

'As long as I was losing to Aaron, my game was improving. Ever since I started winning, only my ego improved, my game did not.'

You need better opponents, not more wins. You need harder lessons, not more medals. You need to exceed your limits, not merely find them. To be exceptional you need to drive yourself to do what you have not done before. Better to lose against very worthy opponents than to beat a mediocre one.

Life is not always a zero-sum game; business has a very large podium with many medallists. No-one started and stayed at the top in a competitive field. To get better you would need to fight fiercer dragons more frequently.

There are many more losses than wins. Everyone will lose at least once in the tournament except the eventual single winner. There's one World Champion in a sport – temporarily. Hot streaks indicate great progression but only 13 world champion boxers ever retired unbeaten. Losing against better opponents should not only carry lessons but also inspire you to become a better winner.

42.

SPEAK TO MY NEED, NOT OFF YOUR SCRIPT

Conversing with a good friend is a pleasure beyond description – no wonder we long for the company of fellows above all other spiritual needs. When the soul is opened and well-received, we feel that we're godly and made to enjoy life on earth.

An honest, straight and insightful conversation on a topic that brings description, insight and usefulness is probably the reason the Creator gave us a tongue, a voice-box and two ears. Time stands still when words are music to the soul and we're so much richer in its afterglow. Why cannot we have these sort of connections in the boardroom, around the negotiation table or even in a sales call?

Do not talk to me off your script, talk to me as a trusted friend and say the things I will find important and enjoyable. Let me bask in your rendition of superior knowledge that burns away my ignorance. Enrich my understanding and make me want to listen to whatever else you want to say. My time is as precious as yours so please prepare an oration, not a lecture; sprinkle me with wisdom, not issues and I may want to forge a long and prosperous relationship.

43.

Hidden hierarchies

Office hierarchies are deep – to the last person – are in flux and are fought over constantly. These informal alliances and got-your-back do not mirror corporate structure. The human drive of self-preservation and ganging-up is extraordinary in good times and even stronger under pressure.

There are gangs around the office that you may only be dimly aware of. Task a couple of confidants to map the associations and hierarchies independently, without each knowing about the other. Compare. Be amazed. Understand that you're the provider, not the benefactor and your cushy seat may be someone else's, soon, if you're not the dominant player.

Be careful who you support or shun without valid and well-articulated reasons. Once you know who leads the packs you can manage a path to influence better. The power structures may ebb and flow but the allegiances stay, so make this knowledge work for you.

44.

LOOK TO SEE

Eidetic: [adjective] marked by or involving extraordinarily accurate and vivid recall especially of visual images.

This is you, right? We hear with our eyes as our ears can't reach to the horizon. Once the captions are turned on, the audio on the TV becomes background. If you do some EyeGym, (eyegym.com) your acuity and perception ability will increase dramatically. We are visual creatures above all other senses. It is by far the most accurate and important of the ways to take in your surroundings – including intuition and otherworldly claimed gifts.

The Unconventional in you must develop eidetic vision to remember what you perceive, see, understand and mark as important. Not only must you watch, but also understand what's playing out around you; from micro expressions to body language, from group interaction changes to unusual interpersonal set-ups.

Your eyes must warn you ahead of time, you need to learn to look for meaning and changes and then remember what you saw: who, where and why, from faces to documents. Notice the new shoes, the change in phones; signs of new wealth or insubordination. Look to see, to understand and to remember, sharp eyes are your best ally and your first line of defence.

45.

CHOICE WORDS

Obloquy: [noun] a strongly condemnatory utterance.

As an Unconventional sharer of business wisdom, you should have an unique set of words and phrases that convey meaning. A handful of studied gestures, postures and verbal signs should give a clear indication that either CV's should be updated or champagne opened.

The obvious do not need gilding or flaying; your silent stare with one raised eyebrow should convey the History of Rome from its start to the fall thereof. The object of your stare should understand that no further words are required until his departure with a small box of personal items. Ditto expressing your famous phrases with a nodding head and smiling eyes: world-cup winning celebrations to follow after the crowning ceremony.

Be a minimalist. Time is precious to you and your loyalists. Don't restate the obvious, you need to express your understanding of the situation, its consequences, the correct plan of action and the high possibility of its success in a single heart-warming shrug. Get it known that you crave the essential and like to hear it in short lucid sentences too. At any conclusion everyone should know where you stand before by your single reaction. Have that one word that means 'disaster' and another meaning 'beers all around'. Be a legend.

46.

Businessman as an athlete?

Getting stronger requires a different technique than just maintaining fitness. So does getting faster, and in a competitive team sport like business, it means revising all the aspects needed to overcome other teams by a better own performance.

If you look at yourself as an athlete competing all day long you will have to find the time to get better at what you do. Will you take on a coach or a new training programme? Define your weaknesses and set time aside to think through remedials and then train to a higher standard.

At best most office jocks only compete and rest. The objective analysis of the game, identifying the causes of the mistakes, thinking through alternative strategies and evaluating the outcome on a measurable basis are alien to most.

How would you set up an Unconventional way of evaluating the plays and games? Who will officiate and who will help you and your team get constantly better at what you're doing? Spending forty hours a week on a tennis court under tutelage should vastly improve your game – imagine this over 30 year career! Your office game is no different.

Set up your get-better programme and canvass your team to participate. It may not be blood sport at the office, but it will be the longest and hardest game you'll ever play. Get better at it every day, champ.

47.

WISDOM OF OLD PEOPLE

This is not true. Wisdom and old people do not equate, at best old people can rediscover old wisdom and pass it on. Young people can do this too but may not recognise the unearthed jewels for what they are.

Age narrows the options and choices but it also allows one to declutter the experiences into heaps of either nonsense or wisdom. In general, things that have lasted a longer time has more value. Hats don't, socks do. Cashflow does and ESG reporting does not constitute business wisdom.

Scratch away the accumulated embellishments to expose the shine; distil and concentrate down to the essence of the idea. Test your concept and pass it on once you're satisfied. Start doing it now and don't wait for the 'someday'

48.

EARLY ON THE BRAKES IN TROUBLE, HARD ON THE GAS IN GOOD TIMES

Driving fast differs from steering an organizational behemoth in multiple ways. The latter may have no easy gear changes, a very slow response to the yank on the steering wheel and of course, a pretty steady pace that will hardly blow any manager's hair back.

The behemoth has its own momentum and responds much quicker to the brake than to acceleration attempts. This is an excellent set-up; companies at speed go maybe 3% net profit on sales per annum despite the supercharger and turbo being pushed to their limits.

The brake pedal is the best way of keeping the structure safely on the road and moving steadily. There are more obstacles than opportunities and hitting one may be more damaging than the benefit of a year's worth of just speeding up.

When the tail starts coming out around a difficult corner, a quick correction will make for an exhilarating slide. However much the team talk is of ripping around the circuit, the prudent Unconventional would rather grab the handbrake early than to count the cost of collision with a nasty object like a cash crunch or a production cost overrun.

Paint the GT stripes at the earliest opportunity but prudently brake well before the crash barriers.

49.

The suitcase carousel question

You may assume that everyone – at least most people – are rational, and you will be mistaken. You would be the one waiting by the carousel at the closest point where the suitcases exit. Why isn't everyone so concerned about saving time and effort? Why the irrationality?

Some cars hold their value well and others become rust buckets without resale. The range of different vehicles in your corporate car park displays a set of purchasing decisions spanning rational to sheer stupid choices. Part of your job is to make absolutely sure that none of that irrationality is displayed inside the building.

Needless stupidity is a topic for your pep talks and the examples can be limitless. When the Dunning-Krügers start thinking before doing, your stop & fix ratio should plummet. Test for the numbers of re-quotes, journal entries, returns to stores, re-invoicing and missed appointment and then crack the whip.

Most people get paid by time and mistake-fixing in that time is an expensive waste. A Deming's-type 'zero-mistake' culture should aid everyone involved to up their game. This type of behaviour should carry over into their personal lives too. Soon you may see only white Toyotas parked outside.

50.

Mental Toughness test

How much resilience is good? When should resilience be traded for adaptability? One mental toughness test checks 5 factors to determine the can do/will do factor that separates the exceptional one's from the participation medallists. This Mental Toughness score matches the primary traits of adaptability and resilience with two more factors to calculate a person's MT profile.

Short of sending your high-flyers crawling under low barbed wire, while ducking live fire, you would like to know how they would perform under severely and extended stress. Better to know than to hope and best to prepare for what you know. In essence you want to see unflustered grit. That's what Marine boot camp and other elite soldier selection test for, plus a little body toughness too.

Your cadres should display high levels of adaptability – the calmness, bounce-back ability thinking laterally in unknown situations. This trait is underscored by self-control of emotions, desires and distractions. Optimism in the face of adversity shows control of a situation with steadfast hope that the answers exist and need to be found.

On the 'tough' side, persistence rules. Working through frustration and without time limits isn't an easily learned characteristic. Adversity does not build persistence, it merely reveals it – like character. Your mental Marine should be fairly calm and driven to finish the disagreeable disaster at hand, when so required.

How would you score? Will you test your shock troops and how would they stack up? What will you do with those who fail your expectations?

51.

FRAMING A PREJUDICE FIRST BEFORE THE OTHER PARTY DOES

You might find that some people are impossible to pry away off their prejudices. Some people snap to these biases like an alligator – never to release again. Those who take an instant dislike to your idea – or to you – are hard to convert unless you fancy yourself an reptile whisperer.

Many amateurs prowling the business world have a tenuous grip on their emotions and slip from being professional to playground idiocy of puffed cheeks. Armed with the expectation that this behaviour may scupper a seemingly prosperous avenue, you should snap to a defensive strategy first.

You need to pre-empt prejudice with some of your own. What's needed is a positive prejudice with a backdoor. Your opposite number is going to be an astute businessman, benevolent to a fault, overflowing with good instincts and a great person to boot. This is your mindset, all the while expecting that he is really none of the above but you are giving him every reason to great until he proves that he should be booted out.

With such a warm expectation you may disarm his snapping tendencies and if you don't, you were probably meant to be on the menu.

52.

COLLECTIVE ILLUSIONS

Be wary of any trumpeted ideology. Not only is it usually an ill-defined catch-phrase for a jumble of ideas, but it shoehorns variations and improvements into a memory hole. Socialism? Capitalism? CRT? All catch-all phrases that cannot bear strong scrutiny.

Collective Illusions are situations where most people in a group go along with a view because they incorrectly believe that most people, or most in the group, agree with that view. It feeds itself. Stolen election? One world government? Inherent racism? When no debate is tolerated , the questioners are stigmatised and dissenters marginalised. Worse, there is surely a minority view touted and hammered into minds that becomes such a collective illusion.

Media is infamous for introducing news stories from a single person's perspective as if it is a majority view. There could be some collective illusions in your wagon train as well. Flatteringly, some might think you walk on water and most would assume others think so too. More seriously, expectations and beliefs could be that your systems are invulnerable to hacking, that there is ample credit lines at the Bank and HR's training programme is boosting productivity.

Obviously not all CI's are bad – as long as you understand what is true and what is just corporate ideology. It is good that those manning the trenches believe the indestructibility of the cashflow and the invulnerability of their CEO. Best not to tell them otherwise for now but you should selectively allow your starry-eyed to question the important assumptions. Leave ideology to the politicians.

53.

Light but Fast

How perfect must your decisions be? Are your willing to create a situation where the imperfect is tolerated?

The basic premise of this 'LBF' strategy is that making faster decisions that are imperfect but mostly correct is better than making slower decisions that are perfect because it forces your competitors to react to you instead of the other way around.

As a result, you can control the pace of the market, engagement, publicly, while your competitors are forced to adapt to your moves. While perfection is in your mind, you must play the shots without losing momentum.

54.

'STRATEGY WITHOUT TACTICS IS THE SLOWEST WAY TO VICTORY' – SUN TZU

There's a fair bit of militarism splashed about in the previous volumes. War by combat is the failure of other means of domination and persuasion. Many have written about the good implementation of resources, optimum engagement with reams of interpretation. Here is a slant on that.

Strategy is only feasible if it can be executed in a variety of on-the-fly adaptations. Like economics, many stable aspects are assumed; the roads are passable, the ammunition can be replenished, the intelligence is correct and complete, the enemy will react or act in certain containable ways. Strategy is adaptable – if the new adaptation can be implemented.

Tactics must not only be adaptable but must maintain the needed level of efficiency to execute the strategy. Your marketing campaign kicks off for the wonder widget. The assassination of the President grabs the headlines. How do you still get your message across? The plan B, C and D must exist, be known and be implementable without a whiff of panic.

The depth of planning for a possible setback and changed circumstances will determine your momentum. The battle is slow and grinding. Even *Generaloberst* Guderian's tank charge through the Ardennes took 45 days. Adaption, improvement, crisis, choices, fallback, adaption… repeat. All this while holding firm to the strategy. A changing strategy multiplies the number of tactical executions. Fail on these – and start anew.

As Sun Tzu completes the quote – and which is often omitted: 'Tactics without strategy is the rumbling noise before defeat'.

55.

BIG-ITIS

Be leery of those who cloak their failures as almost-successes; done deals except they will close 'any day soon' and so on. If the narrative says that salvation lies in the BIG deals they are working on, it's time to move them on.

Big-itis is the incompetent's way to buy time with your enthusiasm while updating CV's on the sly. Big leaps are for losers and wanna-be's. Like true love they might strike unexpectedly – and perhaps once in a lifetime. Big deals are done by people to whom these aren't big deals but normal fare.

Your enthusiastic badger fancies cornering a buffalo and you know that only lions lunch there. Sometimes honey badgers nip off the testicles of a young bull but that leads to gelding growth and not a badger family feast. Your salespeople are comfortable in a band of deal-sizes. Dealing smaller is an insult but in trying for the big game trophies they might not have enough calibre in their guns.

Gently dissuade them from betting only on that, it is akin to poaching on another's turf. Best to find the veterans who roam those paths with casual ease, knowing their deal-size limitations and delivering steady streams of success.

56.

SMALL-ITIS

It's basic human nature to gyrate to the easy and procrastinate the urgently big. Dealing with a smaller framed problem instead of the bigger issue means fooling the other side as well as yourself.

The spectre of small-itis will sink its teeth into anatomically embarrassing parts if you don't stamp on this tendency and grind it to dust. Not only should you view all tasks at hand as Urgent or Important (described in a previous chapter) but also conversely as Big Issue or Nuisance.

Better grit the chompers and go stop the invasion now rather than to fret about the fit of your boots. In a list of 50 to-do's, the square thereof will be the Big & Important; find those seven top items and trash them right away. This habit must cascade down to the juniors; perhaps their daily lists to-do must be shown around before morning coffees and judged at knock-off time for the amount of 'done' ticks.

The ability to recognise that which will have the largest impact on survival and prosperity is a fine skill. This must be taught, honed, tested for and rewarded. Lead the way, report your wins publicly and demand a chorus of similar victory chants. Urge your guardians to do the Big Things first, not to get caught up wasting time on the small stuff.

57.

AGREEMENT PRECISION

It is a nightmare to draw up the legal papers to sue on the misunderstood and breached contract. The general remedy is to first waterproof the agreement by multiple layers of lawyers. The other side's game is to undo your stickiness and insert their landmines and the result may often – very, very often – be half a tree's paper that rivals the Pentateuch in width, complexity and of course, interpretation.

This tango of the *Consiglieri's* can undo the deal, spread permanent suspicion and damage reputations. No-one wants to come out of a failed negotiation radiating deadly kryptonite. No-one wants to realise that a major loophole was created and signed off either. Legally, being prudent racks up eye-watering professional hours. From a commercial understanding to a legal bind is a painful and a crawl on broken glass may be preferable.

A deal is made up of 3 parts, and in order of importance: (a) what are we exchanging and why are we doing it?; (b) what feudal punishments do we include as penance to make sure we collaborate on solving misunderstandings; and (c) the rest of the legal doodles that bulk up from copy & paste standard wordings.

The crisis involves the four parties, you, them and the two separate lawyer teams. Perhaps the answer is to split the responsibility between the two legal teams; yours do (a) above and they get to do (b); the (c) part is anyone's legal secretary's speciality. Sound like the kid's game of you-divide-then-I-choose-first. This also halves the cost (and the fees) so be firm.

58.

INTELLIGENCE AND INTEGRITY

Having both these two attributes is the best predictor of long-term success. For an additional boost a helping of selflessness, humility, ruthlessness and of course, unconventionality, can shoot a higher arc of your stellar ambitions.

Quite a number of 'intelligences' have been defined; from spatial to emotional. The particular traits of quick-grasping, association-making and consequence-understanding underlie this form of mental acuity. The latter two can be exercised and improved and scoring high here is more important than the Stanford-Binet mark.

Microsecond fast reactions are rarely required during business hours and cooled-down responses are invariably safer. These two traits must be foremost on your list for vetting your helpers, from start to promotion. How will you conduct yourself? In a rule-based world you should still follow your best intentions and behave scrupulously. You might be amongst snakes, but you could have them for dinner.

Work on your knowledge and on stamping your principles on everyone around you. In building your success around these two elements, bear in mind that the first can be polished but that the latter may only be irretrievably lost.

59.

INDIRECT WARFARE

The best way to stop a tank from your fighter airplane is to overfly it and knock out its support group hauling the extra fuel, ammo, spares and crew. The tank will be helpless in no time.

It is difficult to win a fight against a bigger guy when standing toe to toe. The best warfare is not waging war on the enemy's troops, but on his alliances, plans and ability to do combat. Heroes are targeted in return and need extra protection to survive.

The anti-hero avoids the slugfest where possible, his strategy is to win and not to merely posture. Indirect business warfare ideas can stretch the limits of your imagination thereof.

In Namibia, we once recruited the whole sales team of the dominant school books seller a week before schools placed their orders. Checkmate. With a major telecoms provider we negotiated cumulative airmiles which we used to incentivise resellers away from the opposition. It peaked at a staggering 13 million miles. We moved into the building opposite the best fibre connectivity vendor to mix with their executives daily at the only restaurant in the vicinity. We got first dibs at things on offer.

Indirect warfare may be cheaper and more effective that hand to hand combat and a lot more fun to manifest. Go and be Unconventional!

60.

PRESSURE

How does one "manage people"? You could feed, inoculate and breed cattle for offspring but people? Let's assume your interest in daytime is restricted to getting the best out of who you're paying. Manage their tasks? Manage their time? What exactly would you do amongst a group of trained, motivated and incentivised grafters?

So this is another woolly concept , the 'peace on earth' version of management. Once you've properly set up and pointed the starlings towards their nirvana, step out of their way. Do you want to solve their issues? How else will they learn and grow? After setting the parameters and the feedback measures, it's game on and no coach allowed on the playing field.

Good managers don't attempt to manage people. They manage pressure – these points of contention, frustration and irritation that are pebbles in the boots. Those who can alleviate pressure points to maintain low tension in any domain are rewarded by a group of integrated and highly optimised men.

The 'manage' job becomes sweeping the trails before the pack cycles past at breakneck pace; hot towels between shark dives and well-scouted terrain when hunting the buff. The calm untying of the intertwined knots, preparation of the tools required and soothing the emotions from misunderstandings is where the manager's shadow must fall.

Pressure should be generated by the guys and girls jostling for the best opportunities. Pressure must be managed and directed, not eliminated, else the only rewards fall to the liquidators.

61.

PELOTON

Your industry competes for a slice of all the business purchases made and your sales force fights for a piece of that pie. In a cycling peloton, all riders gets benefit from reduced drag when drafting behind the leader. Your peloton is one of many on the National GDP track.

When the opportunity arises, tuck in behind the lead rider in front and save your effort for a later overtake. Clients hardly compare the posturing and egos of vendors; most products meet a need well enough established. This is cemented tight with a generous helping of trust.

Effort alone won't dislodge an existing rival's relationship so buckle up – few sellers sell ALL their products to every client. Find the loose brick and pry it loose for a foothold in a relationship that may expand. Save your energy until it's time to strike for the yellow jersey.

War room thinking and a peloton execution is a good combination in approaching new clients. You would have to defeat some other alliance soundly – what is the plan? So draft while it is being rolled out and set-up, and get close to the opposition to see their execution. Wait for the opportune moment to shoot past for the podium place.

62.

WHO HAS PROVED YOU WRONG?

Hats off to the brave disagreeables who put their money where their mouths are. It's a special kind of hormonal flush that brings out the challenge in a subordinate. Are you encouraging this rare behaviour? You should. The exact the words of challenge you should use: 'prove me wrong by Thursday'.

It works as follows: set the scene for a duel of conclusions that can benefit all parties. This provokes critical thinking and tests established outcomes in a managed setting. There's no punishment for participation, no shaming of the ballsy ones, only critical discussion of the proof.

What kind of challenge? "We can cut financial service expenses by 50% in 12 months. Who argues for, who against? Then set them free.

It is not a zero sum game – some elements might be accepted on merit. The game isn't to prove you wrong but to confirm or to change to the best practises possible. In time, these will become 'our' methods and your young lions would have cut their teeth on safe bones.

63.

INCREMENTALS

Great ideas may grab you by the throat in a single sentence. Fleshing out the details require more words, paragraphs, detail, sketches and discussion. "Going to the moon before the decade is out" was incrementally developed over uncountable sessions until the splashdown of Apollo 11.

Such incrementals must be documented step by step to solidify the structure on which the details will hang. Tedious and painful as it may be, overenthusiasm can ruin the logical limit of benefit. Moon? Why not Mars or Alpha Centauri? Nice talk but it detracts from the focus on the job at hand, land a man and bring him safely back from the Sea of Tranquillity.

The detailed incremental's allows for a roll-back from a dead-end to the last and valid assumption. Documenting the path will make a future audit for improvement possible and effective. The relationship between complimentary and symbiotic systems can be measured. Most of all, you may be able to understand the steps of progress too if the engineers and marketeers do the process well.

64.

RUNES AND REPUTATIONS

Vikings set great store by their achievements and their next of kin often erected the runestones to tell those who came after of their exploits. That's a reputation set in stone. Its either rune or ruin and it's your choice.

Some say that retirement offers a chance to revisit all the accumulated reputational disasters with time in hand to repair them. It would be a sad day to sneak away to fix even a single one, but who will cast the first stone? In meeting his Majesty for your Knighthood, he is not going to ask how much you earned or who you vanquished, you'll be on one knee because your excellent reputation preceded you.

What will your runestone tell your progeny? A tale of adventure, achievement and the honours befitting a Great Man? Start carving it right away, make it legendary and may it give you great satisfaction that you will be leaving this world old and broken, but it a far better place.

65.

THE HERO'S JOURNEY

Joseph Campbell postulated that all myths have a very similar structure. Heroes, reluctant or not, follow the path from the uninitiated known world through the catharsis of experiences in the unknown to return as the master of both these worlds – if he returns.

Surely you set out with your first steps in business to retire with the Laurel wreath around your shoulders and a heavy, shining pendant hanging around your neck. If you only knew the trails and tests awaiting you! The monsters, temptations and ordeals that will transform not only your knowledge but your deepest being would make you a little more wary.

When looking back, you would recognise the thresholds you crossed and the resurrections your experienced. It wasn't easy and Business Studies don't include directions on this map to your success. Take the time to prepare your own future heroes for the journey while understanding why yours took those bumpy turns too.

66.

IF YOU WANT TO TRAIN A GOOD LONGBOWMAN, START WITH HIS GRANDFATHER

Some skills are generationally long in the making. Dynasties often succeed or fail on the handing down and the uptake of skills. Entrepreneurship is not easily taught or learned. The 'nose' for business and opportunities can rest on a set of demonstrated and frequently reinforced deeds. The requirements for a successful business change over time. At the time of generational handover some of acumen may be unrecognizable but still relevant – like choosing a personal banker.

Some life skills become as important as business skills. These aptitudes include patience, the ability to defuse situations, seeing through trickery, attracting and keeping good staff, reading market trend in time, prioritising correctly and spotting deviancy early. Most of these are honed by watching an expert in action and guesswork is absolutely out of the question.

It is expensive to have the newbie learn these skills on your payroll; good habits and good sense should be learned at home from parents who learned that too. Those with the good fortune of learning from solid business role models have immeasurable gains over the neophytes in their profession. Combining good life skills and real institutional understanding is beyond price. The sins of neglect though is truly shown in the 3rd and 4th generation thereafter.

67.

CHANGING THE GAIT

It is fascinating to learn that different horse breeds have differing gaits. Surely all horses can walk, gallop and run? Genetics determines that a handful of breeds have special abilities, so-called gaitedness. Amongst trot, canter and sprint there are also pace, amble and various forms of rack.

Humans don't have that specific DMRT3 gene expression but most of us do revert to natural tendencies when faced with career aspiration, deadlines and difficulties. We do our own little paces under pressure.

Some display their own gaits. If measurements are unflattering, they simply produce a new number to offset the problem. Else something more self-pleasing to display. Want cashflow and getting working capital? Sales invoiced and getting orders placed? You're being gaited and it didn't even hurt. The offending corruptor may have moved on from that meeting or even that position.

Exact and uncompromising requirements may be what you always expect. Gaitedness isn't a disaster, just know the tendency of some under pressure. After all you are in charge of your horsepower, make sure the gears run on the same way without the fancies outpacing the halter or halt the progress.

68.

COMMAND OR CONTROL?

Military Academies focus on developing a command personality in their new officers turnout. This command is light on detail and requires the application of position power. In contrast, control management is the Business School's answer to better and increased people output. Is there a sweet spot between the two styles? In lazy references, the two terms are interchangeable and worse – conjugated.

The 'command and control' is a know-it-all term that subverts not only the language but the strategic meanings too. In short shrift; command is giving orders while control is making sure these get done. It's the prequel to 'leadership vs. management'. The inferences are top vs. middle management; strategic vs. tactical or organizational vs. operational.

Staff vs. Line – where does the unconventional wisdom implement the overlap between C&C? You could find yourself back at the delegation vs. abdication illustration; and the bottom-up knowledge vs. the office recluse example. Best to understand what you are delegating, an over-the-shoulder peek should satisfy you that the progress is in the correct direction. Not knowing this distinction makes you an armchair General with abdication – without knowing whether progress is real or the difficulties encountered are only imaginary

Napoleon won more battles than anyone else in history – 56. That's 17 more than the Duke of Wellington, his nemesis. He still lost 5 of his eight wars and the 7 most important battles. A total of 1,4 million French casualties including some 500,000 dead in the logistics nightmare of the Russian campaign was the price. Lots of command. Disastrous control.

Your command should have a grasp of the progress of the control. You need the line guys to execute and your staffers to plan. Get legendary for finding the sweet spot there.

69.

NESTED IDENTITIES

Who are your people actually? In modern parlance, this is a loaded question with all kinds of strange implications. 'Nested identitiy' seems like one of the newspeak bastard kids, some term that darkens instead of illuminates. For the unconventional, it means that those deserving to be on the payroll have far, far more complicated their identities than a decade ago.

You may have Rapper Gangstas in tech uniforms who are also Pentecostal Christians. Some are master bakers who call on debtors in the daytime and are Game of Thrones binge watchers. The number of additive identities that can be and are compartmentalised is staggering beyond your best guestimate. The rapidity of change, adoption and enactment is a feature of the digital-access age's persona – the person with many nested identities.

Some are sensitive to gender issues, others are designer drugs aficionados and you would be none the wiser to that when casually asking about the progress of their kids. Homo sapiens is capable of many multiples, from identities to personalities and can be in constant flux. It affects productive behaviour and finding common ground for motivating to achievement is fragmented.

Consider what the 'office of tomorrow' will look like when half of the young people are 'kidults' and do not share your set of values, beliefs, norms, virtues or morals that you hoped to find. It will require unconventional means to gently rope them into productive economic participation, so good luck with helping them to feather their nesting.

70.

'WHAT ARE YOU REALLY CAPABLE OF?'

This is a question that you should frequently and sincerely pose while looking your adjutants squarely in the eyes. Best you write their answers down too. At the next question time, they should have had time to shed the skin of modesty and up their self-expectations. Few would dare to regress, your hope is that the answers get clearer and more detailed every time you ask.

Whipping out your notebook to remind them of the previous answer and pose the question again: 'Bob, what are you *really* capable of?' Yes, it's a job interview every time and it zero-rates itself. It's up to Bob to clarify his aspirations to himself and to his boss. It could become self-fulfilling, a moving target and leave you witnessing professional growth to your astonishment and delight. Who knows what capabilities lurk in the hearts of men?

Your follow-up question once you're satisfied, should reveal even more: 'Bob what can I do to help you get there?' After such satisfying interludes, get ready to meet the man in the mirror that wants to know the same about you. Don't disappoint him.

71.

Un-solveables

A para-religious belief, that bad occurrences are just problems to solve, will destroy us. There are many annoyances that defy solution and do so for diverse reasons. Given enough time, money and effort this list may be shortened but perhaps your calling was to excel in that happy confluence where things that matter are under your control.

Let go of wanting to control the weather. Or people's sexual proclivities. Homelessness. Or the red tape in certain industries. As science progresses, people presume that more issues will be solved. Perhaps so, but not necessarily by you. In your own domain there will be hands-full of intractable issues. Sometimes just containing them is a better time-wise.

Conserve your energy for steady progress and the occasional opportunity to do the exceptional. Let the un-solveables be challenges for the more courageous or foolish. You can't stop your wagon for every menacing dog that barks.

72.

INFORMATION VS CONCLUSION

A closed mind is a terrible waste and even more so if it's on your side of the trench in your best squad. One of the deadly signs of the closed-minded is that they speak in conclusions. The answer is known. The die is cast. Everyone knows that. Tried that, didn't work and so forth. Ask a difficult question and the firm concluders answer with a conviction that will be difficult to move. There is a mass of ego tied to the answer.

This is not good and not what you want. It is better that questions are viewed an invitation to debate instead of being foregones. Life comes at you fast. The world is spinning at 35,000 km an hour on its axis while racing 300,000 km per hour around the sun –things change a lot in very little time. Whatever is known must be revisited often and with vengeance. The scientific methods applies to business as well.

You want answers with information, opinion, tentative conclusions and admitting of room for error. The lid must be opened to think out of the box. Why not … what if … assume that … are the probing starts to flaying the dead skin off a set idea. Conclusions might have been valid for that moment in time when it was reached. Buggies became Tesla's, stamps became data bundles. Don't let the can-not's become should-have's. You don't want conclusions, you require open minds.

73.

LIKEABILITY + COMPETENCE MATRIX

The 4-outcome matrix has been a favourite of the Business School crowd since Boston Consulting popularised it in the '80's. For some fun, let's apply it to the above.

- Not likeable and not competent: bad fit and bad performance, please send that CV to the competition.
- Not likeable but competent: the Lone Ranger with uncertain promotion prospects.
- Likeable but not competent: the Mascot that needs training or a shove towards the exit.
- Likeable and competent: the star of the show.

This shows how easily a classification matrix can be set up to link preferred values and in a way that staff can visualise your expectations. How about sales vs. salaries? Cash vs. investment? The desirable answer is always flanked by unwanted answers for all to see.

74.

COMPETITIVE TYPES
ARE DISAGREEABLE

Following on from the above, the interpretation of likeability is an art and never absolute. If you require harmony, you may end up with mediocrity by yes-men. Should the adventurer in you aim for new horizons, a less agreeable chins will jut out at you: the competitive type.

You must embrace this and the struggle is on; them against you. It will require energy, craftiness, confidence and a fair bit of luck disguised as authority to drive those wild horses in front of the chariot and not fatally drop the reins. Lion males in a pride jostle for position and often brutally so.

Disagreeable-ness is part hormonal and also deadly – for you or the competition. You will have to earn its respect – constantly. Position power is only a temporary poultice, to be the main lion you have to do lion things too, not just roar in their ears. Hunt as a pack and overcome, else expect hunger to boil over into dissatisfaction and bloodshed.

75.

PROCESS OR OUTCOME? WEST OR EAST?

An organisation often agonises whether it is only results that matter. Where shortcuts are taken, unconventional methods used or plain rules broken to ring the bell first or best creates, a dilemma exists. The losers may cry foul over the Boss's erroneous congratulatory whoops. Shouldn't everyone colour in between the lines and achieve in the preconceived and agreed methods?

On the one extreme, such cheating behaviour is reprehensible and unfair and should be punished as it makes a mockery of good order and discipline. That's a very Eastern philosophy and ubiquitous in the larger and often more disciplined or stagnant corporation. On the other hand, innovation and progress are omelettes that need some eggs to be broken for progress and new standards.

Think Fosbury flop in high jump or dolphin kick in swimming. Both were rule-bending unconventional methods, but with great outcomes. The 'easier-to-ask-forgiveness' psyche is better tolerated in the West and also in smaller, more dynamic companies. The Brits and Europeans are very East in this regards, Queensberry rules and all.

Which approach is best? Perhaps the question should be 'which is better'.

You needs to spell out the elasticity of the boundaries around the achievements you want. Accounting and stores will be tight as thieves on the side where the sun rises. Engineering could be constructive craziness, but not on current projects – a combination of both. For marketing, sales and customer service it is never Groundhog Day. Perhaps you should at least be somewhat informed beforehand of the magnitude of rail-jumping some of the clowns contemplate. Except that they will be Hero's in success. Encourage but moderate else the clash of culture may be deafening.

76.

THE OPTIMISTS DILEMMA: BETTING AGAINST YOUR BELIEF

Summoning a Rainmaker shows at least two things: you believe in rainmaking and that this one will be successful. It's no fun if the eyes are wet as plains remain dry afterwards. The optimist's dilemma is that whenever he states an optimistic outcome, he bets (and risks) not only his reputation but also his beliefs.

What should you do when you think the future is bright? You shouldn't forecast, especially not for the future. Couching your expectations in too many if's and but's waters down your public mojo. The best strategy is projection. Your people need to do the hard lifting and the bacon-hauling; surely expecting optimistic things from them passes the buck nicely?

Temper this temptation with consent. Start wide and narrow down. Surely there's room to grow in the market? All clients are not ours yet? Possible to bring in 4 worthwhile one's? Should 3 months be unreasonable to bag the first two? These become their optimistic projections with gentle workings from the general to the specific.

Probe a bit int what different tactic and manoeuvres will they use to do what's not done before? Would they consent to making these expectations public? Now they're betting with themselves for glory.

77.

DISCIPLINE VS CREATIVITY

There is wisdom in Foucault's description of how medieval torture punishment was transformed during the Enlightenment. He describes how disciplining those who don't keep to the Norms are meted out today in contrast to earlier times. Then, the body was punished, now the mind is under permanent coercions to obey until automatic docility.

The slightest departures from correct behaviour in society is subject to punishment or micro-penalties of deprivation and petty humiliation. Discipline nowadays aims at cultivating an obedient, adaptable, productive, self-regulating, and useful person. It involves continuous comparison between good and bad citizens or what Foucault calls 'normalizing' judgement.

That's what we do in our organizations too: set rules and fiercely patrol the would-be perpetrators. This is not conducive for creativity. It is fair to say we effectively created prisons but expect the inmates to magically fly through the bars in pursuit of ideas and bring these back to the cells. We train obedient people as circus animals for the good of the circus, for 'your safety and well-being'. We cannot and will not tolerate slights and deviancy and are now coerced to not offend nor exclude any amount of tripe thrown at us. How can your eagles escape this cage and be lauded? This is a serious question without an ersatz answer. The left-brain brigade has atomised us to stereotype drones and this constricts our abilities to dream, create and solve.

We are drowning in discipline and rules, for the common good. The intolerance for 'just in case' regulation is choking us – are we doing the same to our crowd? Time to launch a lifeboat! The golden mean between discipline and creativity is elusive. Go and deserve your pay and find it.

78.

FIND HUNGRY SAMURAI

Everyone has a different point to tip from lethargy to motivated. 'Hot buttons' is a plural, who knows what a bit on unconventional probing can reveal about finding them for your crew? Perhaps the salesperson candidate has needs outside and in contrast to a stiff salary? Perhaps you're a farmer with the only food in an area of thieves – unable to afford the high price of protection? Hence you find a hungry samurai.

It is lazy and unexciting to approach business deals and even internal organization by the cookie cutter method. No deal or task is a mirror image of what went before, the fun and profitable exploration of finding a different or unique set of arrangements add experience and more tools to your arsenal.

Money is not a motivator (says the conventional wisdom), perhaps it's the afterthought that fills up the unmet expectation. If you can satisfy the other needs of acknowledgement, power, position, control, status, prospects, risk, future earnings and other trappings and foibles, you may not need to add all the funds budgeted to make the deal or the position work.

Good luck finding that point for everyone in need of a reason to excel. Hungry Samurai can be fed, and then a different need must be met. Those with a Michelin-star appetites require being spoiled. That's a conundrum, they may already know the distance to a better restaurateur too. Get value or give directions.

79.

Armor yourself with an image

You have different persona's, whether you're the Unconventional or not. A different person kisses a kid good-night than one that redeploys a protagonist. Of the many possible facets, a crafty CEO would have polished a very workable professional image of himself to others. For this, you need to take stock and decide what your 'persuasive persona' is going to be like and do so in detail.

You cannot just polish what you have, you need to find the best in you and supplement it with what you may still require. If you watch the best tennis players after match point you will note the studied humility, graciousness in victory and defeat that fits their public's expectation. Never a word in anger or a negative comment come through those lips since McEnroe way back.

It's a different story at the rugby prize-giving, the public want to smell a little up-yours testosterone. Pitch yourself somewhere between these extremes where you can keep it up. List and detail the rules.

Cussing allowed? Emotional outbursts? Cold and lasting anger? Humour? Acting fast? Sharing information widely? Trust actions? Imagine the perfect CEO and become that person. Inspiring? Forceful? Lead form the front? Unafraid of clients and calamities? Brutally honest? List the Do's and Don'ts.

First become less of what you do not want to be. Once that's settled, become what you should. No need to take this persona home though, you instinctively know how you want to be as the best dad in the world.

Does this help? Here's the famed Scipio Africanus, hero of Rome, crafting his persona:

> … when he noticed this anxiety and concern, follow-
> ing an action taken with such impulsiveness, Scipio

called an assembly, and discoursed with such elevation of spirit on his age and the command entrusted to him and the war to be waged, that he again awakened and revived the ardour which had cooled, and filled men with a more assured hope than belief in a man's promise or reasoning based upon confidence of his success usually inspires for Scipio was remarkable not only for his real abilities, but thanks to a certain skill also had from his youth adapted himself to their display, doing most of his actions before the public either as if they were prompted by visions in the night or inspired by the gods, whether because he also was possessed by a certain superstition, or in order that men might carry out without hesitation his commands and advice, as though emanating from an oracular response.

More than that, preparing men's minds from the very beginning, from the time when he put on the manly gown, there was not a day on which he did any business public or private without going first to the Capitol, and after he had entered the temple, sitting down and usually passing the time there alone in seclusion. This custom, which he maintained throughout his lifetime, confirmed in some men the belief, whether deliberately circulated or by chance, that he was a man of divine race and it revived the tale previously told of Alexander the Great and rivalling it as unfounded gossip, that his conception was due to an immense serpent, and that the form of the strange creature had very often been seen in his mother's chamber, and that, when persons came in, it had suddenly glided away and disappeared from sight. He himself never made light of men's belief in these marvels; on the contrary it was rather promoted by a certain studied practice of neither denying such a thing nor openly asserting it. Many other things of the same sort, some true, some pretended, had passed the limits of admiration for a mere man in the case of this youth. Such were the things on which the citizens relied when they then entrusted to an age far from mature the great responsibility of so important a command.

– Titus Livius (Livy), *The History of Rome, Book 26*

80.

NOT YOU BUT THE TASK

Confidence is a fantastic driver towards the chequered flag. Over-confidence is hubris and many stories are told about the crash in nemesis thereafter. What if the heart is pounding under dry lips and the knees knock ever so slightly? Confidence exists on two levels: the Task and the Me.

Preparation is aimed to do the task perfectly. Execution is aimed at doing that preparation perfectly. These two confidences must meet and merge. The best way outcome is eloquently said by Mike Tyson, when he got in the ring: It's not about you, it's about the task. He mastered his feelings of inadequacy, low self-esteem and doubts. These were subsumed by concentration on executing the task he had prepared for in a legendary way. Fans didn't come to see him, they came to watch what Iron Mike did.

The doubts never left him; but he had the confidences by concentrating of the job instead of himself. This preparation and execution paid enormous dividends. That's true professionalism: getting things done without the baggage of self.

Doctors work through gore and soldiers do the unthinkable. You must always concentrate to do what needs to be done, never on what you feel by doing that. Kings were thrown over the ramparts for not doing what Kings must do, even if it led the assault toward a certain doom. Make yours glorious and don't shirk it, valour is the strongest part of your leadership.

81.

REGROUP

There are lulls when the wide-eyed survivors will look at you with a 'what now?' expression. You brought them there, they survived but it didn't positively go as planned. Time for the strategic regroup. There needn't be an Atlantis sinking disaster. Any event that prompts a re-think of direction, motivation and rate of casualties calls for a folded-legs sit down. Then a general contemplation to make sense of the new and unanticipated situation can be made: a regroup.

Frankly you have two choices, Charybdis or Scylla – rock and a hard place for the less animated minded. You can either double down and redo the recent past better, or suggest something different. Your appeal to raise the weary from victim to survivor stands a far better chance should you choose to redo the assault like King Henry at Agincourt; at least this is familiar to the host and surely the effort born from desperation will carry the day.

To start something different is tantamount to admitting defeat on the previous attempt and means undoing the ape-IQ rollback that the stress induced. The almost middle way – but slightly different than before – is the safest path, unless your brainwave for an alternative was inspired by Alexander or Napoleon.

Regroup means factual analysis, perspective by observation and then a with support, a renewed effort. Hopefully after refreshments and a proper prep talk, commitment to the leader may have waivered but they must have confidence in your Plan B. Remember this alphabet is rather short – by Plan C, your successor is already filling in his application form.

82.

YOU CAN ONLY APPEAL TO WHAT'S RIGHT OR WRONG; OR TO CONSEQUENCES

Some decisions flummox us lesser Salomon's. That's why you earn the accolades and the Danger Money that you do. It's not just about strategy or leadership, it's about decisions; one after the other on a continuous double-or-nothing basis. Heads you stay another day; tails you polish the interview skills.

The CEO position is brutal and yet no-one wants to hear about your dilemmas, scrambling, fixes, victories and flaming defeats; your walks on water must be mystical to the mere shore-dwellers. To what compass do you set your decision machinery or do you just lodestone through the mist ever forwards?

Perhaps the two most extreme ways of judging your pending decision is by either morals or outcomes. Either the its Right/Wrong; or What's the consequences? This means either by Principles or by Outcomes. Most of your decisions will be made by the latter method – what will we win/what may we lose? Not only are the consequences a less than predictable outcome but the unintended consequences are unforeseen and incalculable.

Going by the Right/Wrong method isn't any more certain but at least every question re-affirms the base point of origin: this is who we are, is this decision right and right for us or not? There is continued conflict between the methods and the outcomes, often between the obligations and temptations.

Be aware of the two methodologies as your subordinates may lean towards one or the other and you could test their answers with the opposing appeal. Do what's right and fear no-one. This is my personal motto and it has guiding many Vikings before.

83.

Rite of passage

Short of an anthropological investigation, it is necessary to understand the transition from adolescence to adulthood that everyone should make. Unfortunately many do not recognize, realise or get the opportunity to step out of the shadow of the father or mother figure to raise their own self as an equal and, importantly, be recognised by the parent for having done so.

You might have young and perhaps not so sprightly people that have never formed their own independent identities. Their professional behaviour may suffer from this. However pleasing it might be to feel like a respected father in your amblings amongst your flock, you need the Shakespearian Cordelia's of this world to add substance to their and your world.

Obedient followers or disobedient challengers – which group will contribute to the future? In days of yore, compulsory military service, gap years and Peace Corps assignments gave the youngsters time and space to find their real selves.

University residence and other pre-work/after home experience shape their ability to evaluate and confront your Greybeard's ideas of what the world should look like. Test for these abilities and bear in mind that rites of passage should help predict steps into the adult that you would want to nourish. This will be hard on the more timid souls but you need unconventional soldiers, able to start life in your army at a trot.

84.

PLEASURE PEAKS

Like adrenaline, dopamine is a scarce but renewable resource. A great moment may jubilantly drain your glands (actually it's made in the gut) and hand you a proper downer post-partum. You will then crave the upper more – and although it sounds like a real motivator, it can border addiction. High 'up's' leads to lower 'down's and it's while waiting to recharge the endocrines that depression or worse – cravings – start.

Are you mentally strong enough to modulate the highs to avoid the lows? Not the Scrooge flat-liner, but maybe a lengthened enjoyment instead of a wicked spurt?

Pleasure has its price and paying it shouldn't distract from what you expected when pursuing the feeling of the laurel wreath around your shoulders. Sharing the joy should bask all in its diffusing afterglow instead of just a personal me! me! selfishness. After all, didn't anyone at all help you get on the podium?

Go forth and do well. Count the podium finishes of your protégé's as your own – that's Unconventional maturity.

FIN

www.ingramcontent.com/pod-product-compliance
Lightning Source LLC
Chambersburg PA
CBHW022059210326
41520CB00046B/731